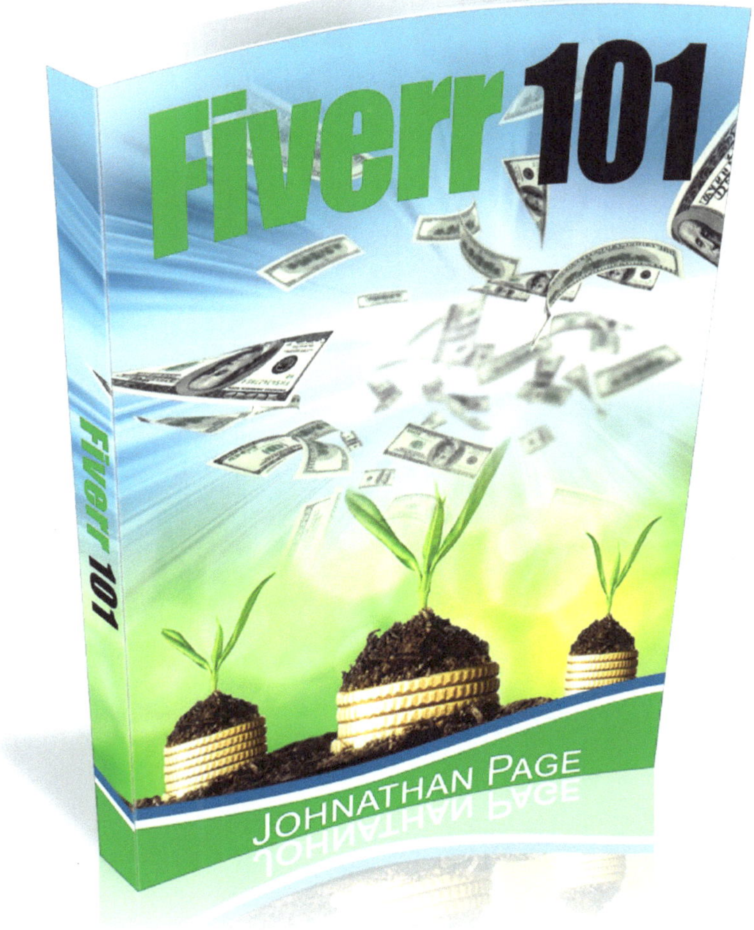

Fiverr 101
Johnathan Page

Outlines

Introduction...3

Getting Started With Fiverr..5

Gig Creation Strategies..8

Ways to Promote Your Gig and Get Orders...............................14

How to Maximize Your Earning...18

How to Get Success at Each Step..24

Summary………………………………………………….
………………….27

Introduction

This book explains about one of the best earning sources through which you can earn easily if you have any skills. Actually, Fiverr helps you to buy or sell different gigs in the form of different mini jobs and services. Whenever a person is new to the online earning system then he or she gets afraid early due to different problems like PayPal issues, networking, social bookmarking and blogging etc. But Fiverr eliminates this problem and helps you to show your skills in an easier way. It can be considered like a platform where people can easily sell and buy their services to or from others who are really experts in their areas. The founders of this site are

Micha Kaufman and Shai Wininger and they launched it in 2009. Now, it is one of the most popular and largest online marketplaces for different services and is available in more than 200 countries. Although, Fiverr service starts at 5$ but it can be extended in to thousand dollars within a month depending upon your skills and the way in which you manage time for it as well as how do you deal with your clients. The site however adds your experience in the form of reviews which helps to show your experience with other clients who really want to get benefits from your services and they can easily trust you depending upon the comments and reviews given to you from other buyers and sellers. The site is primarily used by freelancers and customers who use this platform to offer numerous services and to buy those services respectively.

Just as every person has different skills and can provide different services in an efficient way, the same holds true here. Fiverr is not limited to a single service or the single gig offer but it provides different gigs ranging into thousands or may be more than that. You can also join it and work on it easily if you are a good writer, programmer, designer, web developer, illustrator and editor etc. One of the best and attractive things of Fiverr is that you can sign up free of cost and it is therefore chosen by many beginners who have a zero balance at the beginning. You can start selling your services for 5$ and the Fiverr will take only 1$ each time from it and the remaining 4$ will be added to your account. It means that if you have zero balance during sign up then you will get 4$ each time after selling a service of 5$ and it will give you a unique happiness while getting your first income from an online earning site being a beginner. Those who are expert in their skills and are working at Fiverr for many months can easily earn thousands of dollars by adding extras to their offers. There is no limit of the gigs offered by you and you can easily post as much as you want without any charges. You will get a five star review and a positive feedback each time when you will satisfy a customer with your work and then you will have no more control over feedback or rating. You need to be realistic and adopt a right way while working on Fiverr otherwise your account will be lost temporarily or may be permanently if you will try to adopt a wrong way or sale a false product. However, it takes 14 days to add amount in your funds which provides you a security and makes sure that every transaction is correct.

Getting Started With Fiverr

It is not so difficult to join Fiverr as it follows simple steps and there are no charges for sign up. You can receive your payments easily by using PayPal or Payoneer (Fiverr revenue card) and it is better to create your account first at any of these two before continuing with Fiverr. After that, you need to click on "Join" if you are new and then enter all of your details. After entering all the details, you will have to verify through email confirmation.

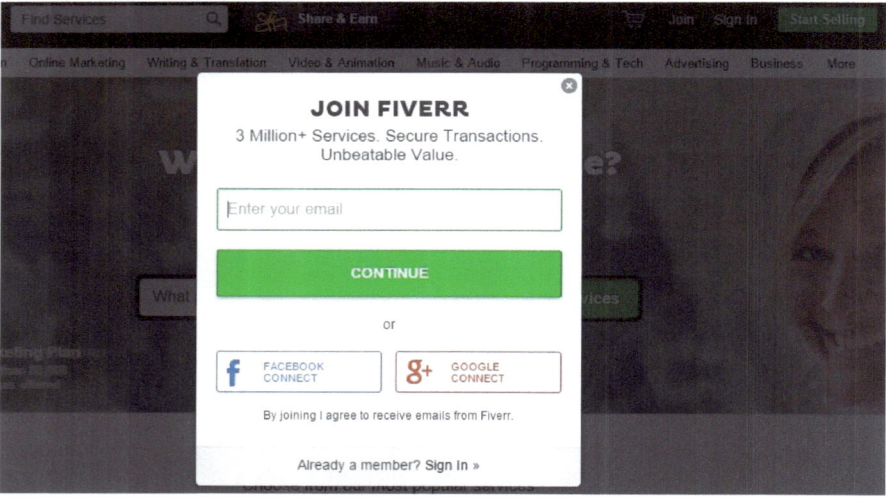

You can also choose your username with the brand of services that you are providing. For example, if you are a good writer then you can select your username as "Writer_guy" or "Writing_expert" and if you are a programmer then you can choose it as "programmer_expert" or "programmer_man" etc. In that case, there will be more chances to represent your services with other clients and your profile can be promoted easily. However, you can also link your profile with Facebook if you really want to introduce this best marketing place with your friends and they will be easily attracted towards this amazing platform when they will see how much you are earning from it.

When you are proceeding for the completion of sign up process then you need to add a good photo of yourself which will show the way of representing yourself on Fiverr and it will play an important role in getting much traffic to your profile. After that you will pass through another section in which you have to describe something about you. This section will show your skills and the area in which you are expert. You can mention your services in a general form in that section and can even share your experience in an impressive way. When the users will read this section then they can also order your services after getting inspiration from the description of this section.

One best thing of Fiverr is that it adds your reviews and rating on the base of previous services that are provided by you with the passage of time. It helps to promote your level depending upon the positive rating and the extent of orders that you have received. You will be promoted to three major stages on Fiverr i.e. level 1, level 2 and top rated seller. Mostly users are likely to select Top rated seller over a level 2 seller and level 2 seller over a level 1 seller.

This level is likely to be given to a user if he is a member for 30 days at least and have completed at least 10 orders with excellent ratings. The advantage of this level is that you are able to offer 2 Gig Extras and users are able to purchase your gigs in multiples up to 4.

This level is likely to be given to a user if he is a member for 60 days at least and have completed at least 50 orders with excellent ratings. The advantage of this level is that you are able to offer 3 Gig Extras and users are able to purchase your gigs in multiples up to 8.

This level is difficult to achieve but it guarantees an enormous traffic to your profile. Such sellers are chosen on the base of seniority, high rating of gigs and good customer services. In this case, you are able to offer 4 Gig extras and users are able to purchase your gigs in multiples up to 20.

Gig Creation Strategies

Whenever you are done with profile then you have to create a gig of your own service. The basic purpose of using an attractive way to create a gig is to get more traffic to your gig so that many people can easily order it. For this purpose different tricks are of great importance like title, image, keywords and category of gig.

First of all, what you need to do is to select the option "Create Gig" and after that you will have to decide a **suitable title** for your gig. The title is the most important thing that attracts a buyer. So, you need to make it clear for your service and the length of the title should be medium. You may also mention the most attractive or unique line of your service in title that may be different from others or you may mention the sale price of your gig if it is less than other similar gigs on Fiverr. A good title may also contain the keywords that are mostly searched by the users. After selecting a title you will pass on to the gig category where you have to choose an **appropriate category** that suits your services. Different categories are popular on a different basis and are searched or visited by users with different proportions depending upon the services which they have. You need to select the right category, otherwise it will not drive the appropriate traffic for your gig.

After selecting a suitable category, you need to add a **cover photo** for your gig which should be related to your services and designed in a best way because it attracts the users towards your gigs. If you are selling a product then the cover photo should be exactly related to what you are selling but if you are providing some sort of services on your own, like voice over or spokesperson then you can add a photo of yourself but the quality of photo should be best and if possible then design it in an efficient way and add some effects to increase its attraction. You can also visit the profile of top rated sellers and can easily check the features of their cover photo.

After adding a unique or an attractive cover photo, you will have to add different photos relevant to your gig in the Gig Gallery. However, this may not be as important as you think, but it gives you an additional bonus in attracting different clients from Fiverr. You can upload different photos in JPEG in the Gig Gallery but their length should be smaller than 2MB and with specific dimensions. This section should also contain high quality photos which may represent the samples of your work. If you are not expert in making a high quality and attractive photos for your gallery then you can hire someone on the Fiverr who can do the same thing for you otherwise you can do it by yourself which will save your money as well. Here is one of the most attractive photos from gig gallery of a top rated seller which can easily provide you a guide to design an impressive photo by yourself or by hiring someone who is an expert in this area.

After uploading different photos in the gig gallery you will pass on to the most important section of gig creation which is the **Gig Description** in which you have to describe the services and the terms in detail. You need to add different keywords in the description or as much as possible so that it can be searched out easily by different users on the Fiverr. The limit is 1200 characters maximum in the description and you can utilize it as much as you can. Your description can be divided into two different parts. In first part, you need to explain the title again and clear every point in it. For next part, you need to add the features of the services which you are providing in your gig. The features can be written in the form of bullets to add an impression for the gig. You must clear everything in this part that what will you offer in your gig for 5$ and can also add the conditions like repetitions or refunding if you could not deliver due to some problems (which is usually optional).

After writing a description for your gig, you need to add the **Tags** for your gig and these are actually the keywords which are mostly searched by the users. The number of maximum keywords that can be added by you is 5 and no keyword can be repeated. Always try your best to put that keyword which is searched by the users of Fiverr. For examples, if you are creating a gig related to YouTube likes then you should add a keyword of "YouTube likes" instead of only YouTube. After adding different tags, you will have to add the **Duration** for your gig which can be selected as the minimum duration if you are a beginner. It will help you to attract the users because they always want their work to be finished as early as possible and with the best quality. So, it is another way to attract them to your services. Next, you need to add the **instructions** for the buyers at the end and you can add different important points for them in this section otherwise it can be considered as an optional thing.

The next section is the most important section for a gig creation which is usually ignored by many of the users due to which they are unable to get many orders. In that section, you will have to upload a **suitable video** which clearly describes the idea of your project. The video should have a medium length less than a minute otherwise it will be rejected by the Fiverr authorities. The most important and best advantage of uploading video is that your gig will move to a higher place in the searches of Fiverr and will not be filtered out when the clients will select only the search option of "video only" for their gigs. From this concept, it is clear that you will not be included in thousands of searches daily when you will not upload a video for your gig.

The chances of getting orders from your gig are increased up to more than 200% after uploading a video. Although it will require some extra effort but it will also increase the number of searches and the visits per day for your gig due to which you can easily get orders from different clients at Fiverr. You have no need to be afraid of any problem that you may face during the creation of a video but you can also take help from different software's like Camtasia Studio, Video Pad, Movie Plus and Windows Movie Maker etc. From these programs, you can easily add different effects in your video and change some boring scenes into attractive animations and transitions. Otherwise, you can also make video by your own if you have a high quality digital camera which can produce better results. If you have no time or you think that you cannot do it in a good way then you can also hire someone at Fiverr who can create a professional video for your gig at average rates. The quality of your video will show how much professional you are in your work.

You can also hire someone out of Fiverr who can design a high quality video of 1 min for you at low rates otherwise if you will ask a person to create a video by his own video makeup who is already on Fiverr then your video can be rejected easily if Fiverr will come to know that it is not your own. So, you need to take a good care to avoid such situation in which you can face the problem like this. Your video should have the following features in order to be more attractive and to get more orders from the clients who are searching for a professional person:

- It should be brief and to the point.
- You need to clear everything in your video and do not add too many pauses which may leave a wrong impression.
- Try to create different videos in a different way for different gigs.

- Mention that your gig is only offered at Fiverr.com and mention your username in the video if possible.

- The length of the video should be within the range of 10 to 50 seconds only.

- You have no need to offer a service other than 5$.

- The quality of video should be very high.

Ways to Promote Your Gig and Get Orders

Whenever you are done with the creation of your gig then the next step is to promote it as much as you can which will help you to increase the traffic for your gig and there will be more chances for getting orders. Some important ways of promoting your gig and getting orders are as follows:

- The first and the well-known place for marketing where you can easily share your gig is Facebook. People from all over the world are present there and you can easily find what they need and can help them through your services. When they will come to know that you are offering your services for only 5$ then they will easily order it as it is affordable. Facebook is the place which contains most of the young generation who can easily divert their likes and dislikes and it is easy for you to convince them towards your services. If they will really like your services then they will order it and will even give you some good reviews. There are different groups at Facebook which are especially used for gigs sharing and promotion. You can also join such groups after searching them and post your relevant services in those groups.

- Next and the important thing for the promotion of your gig is to share your gig at Twitter. As you know, twitter is one of the best marketing places which is usually used by mature people who are really sincere with their profession and already have entered in their practical life. Many of them face little problems some time and you can easily find a solution to their problems in the form of different services of Fiverr and then you can share it with them. If they will like your services then they will also order it and will keep on following you because once you get their trust then they never change their clients and sellers who are providing different services with best quality.

- Another way to share and promote your gig is to share it at **LinkedIn**. As LinkedIn is one of the major platforms that is only meant for the ideas shared by experienced persons and their followers who are supporting or getting benefits from their services. It is a site where professional people are already present and they also need the solution of their problems or promotion of their services and they always support those who help themselves. You can also be one of those and can easily find solution of their issues by introducing a 5$ gig offer through Fiverr and then sharing it with them. In this way, you can get a regular stream of your buyers who will always give you good reviews and will appreciate your services which are being offered by you.

- One more way to share your product is to share it by Google Plus. Whenever you share your gig at Google Plus then it helps Google to promote your gig with respect to its page ranking and you get a universal boost. If you keep on sharing your service at different platforms then it can provide you many opportunities of getting orders.

- One more way to get more orders and to increase the traffic for your gig or service is to go into the option of "My Sales" and then click on "**Buyers requests**". You will see many buyers which are already searching for different users at Fiverr who can help them in the completion of their projects. The numbers of requests which are shown for your profile always depend upon the categories in which you have created your gig. For example, if you have created a single gig of the category "Writing and Translation" then you will get requests of buyers from only that section. So, you need to create all the gigs first related to the categories in which you are expert. After that, you can send them a gig offer or any custom offer if you think that you can easily do their services. For this reason, you need to keep on visiting that page on regular basis because you will find a large number of requests there. Each hour or a day and you need to respond to them on the spot otherwise someone else will send the offer before you which will be accepted by the buyer and you will get nothing.

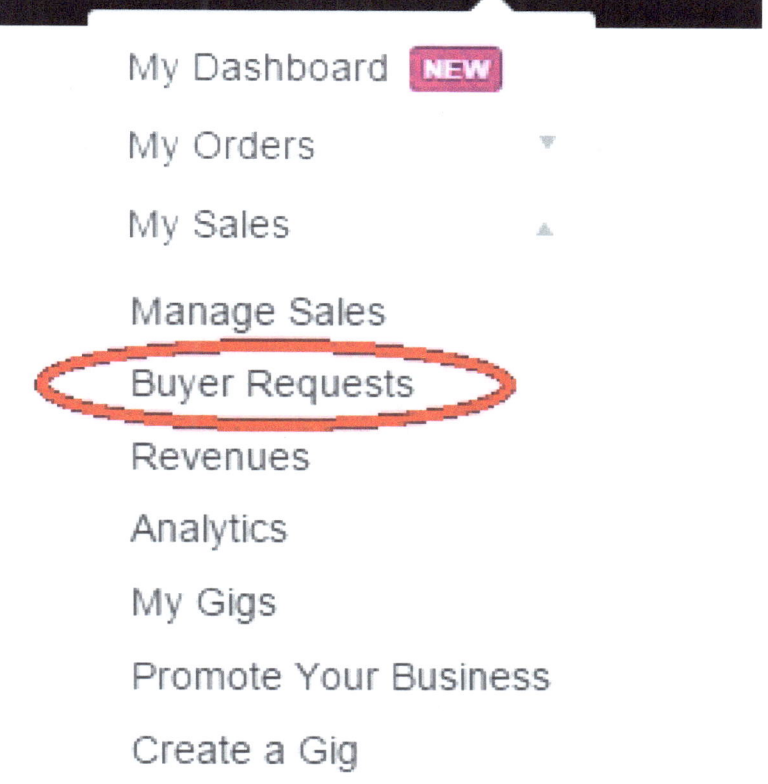

- Another way to promote your gig is to install different software's for the promotion of your products and services but that is not mostly used. You can also install different powerful software's like Buzz Bundle and you will see that it will search the people of all the social media sites related to specific keyword and you can help them after searching for a keyword with a specific service provided by you and can send them requests as well.

How to Maximize Your Earning

Whenever you are working at Fiverr then you need to keep one important thing in mind that you are there to maximize your earning but you can achieve that position only when you will work less for each gig. It does not mean that you should provide the half work to the buyer but it means that you need to be little smart and offer such type of services in which less time is consumed but you can earn good money within small time. For this reason, you need to increase the quality of your services because it is the natural rule that whenever you are selling your product or service then either you need to increase the quantity with respect to price or the quality. So, if you want to earn big money within less time then you need to improve the quality of your services in order to get good reviews and five star rating from the buyer. Some important ways of earning handsome money from different categories of gigs is as follows:

Social Media Marketing

This is one of the most common categories in which every user interested to create a gig because many of the users have no skills at the start and they learn different things with the passage of time at Fiverr. So, it is easy to deliver an order in which you can provide a service related to the Facebook likes, shares, Twitter likes, shares and YouTube Shares etc. For this purpose, you can easily join different online sites for social signaling like addmefast.com that is really providing original likes and shares from different users with exchange methods. Other way is to create your account at seoclerks at which thousands of gigs are available at very low rates even at 1$ or 2$. You can easily buy gigs from that site at low rates and sale them at Fiverr with high rates. In this way, you will have nothing to do except to create an account and wait for a day or two to get a profit.

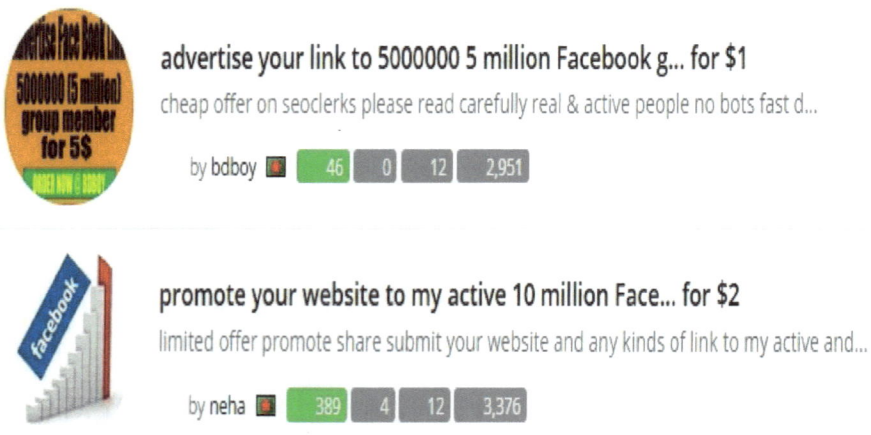

If you have a skill or you know the trick to promote a Facebook page, Twitter profile or a YouTube channel then you can do it by yourself without any cost and the whole amount will be added into your account as your revenue. Otherwise, you can hire different people from seoclerks at low rates who are expert in their field and have been working for such projects throughout the years and you can sale those services at Fiverr with high rates and the result will be the profit. In this way, you can easily assign as much services and can receive different orders in a queue from Fiverr simultaneously which will result in maximum earning within minimum time.

Writing and Translation

This is another section that is preferred by many users who are beginner at Fiverr and know nothing about different tricks. Mostly, people can easily write on different topics easily especially for the fields in which they are expert ranging from 500 to 600 words within an hour. In this way, they can easily earn 5$ from a gig at start after writing a unique and an attractive content of 500 to 600 words. You may also increase the words limit at start up to 1000 words to get more orders and after getting reviews and the promotion of your level, you can easily reduce the words limit per gig. If you are not able to write enough words within a day then it does not mean you cannot maximize your earning. You can easily hire different users from other freelancing sites at low rates like upwork and seoclerks and then can easily deliver your order at Fiverr at high rates. Although, it is time consuming but it does not consume more than that time which will be wasted if you start writing for every gig by your own and it will also help you to earn maximum profit within a minimum time. Through these tricks, you will not only be able to earn more money but you can also get many orders at a time and can easily manage their delivery on time. You may also edit the content if you need where it is necessary otherwise you will have to just receive from only side and transfer it to the other side and you will get a good profit in return.

Videos and Animation

This is another important section but it is not usually chosen by the beginners but you can do it if you know the trick how to work in this area. One of the best gig in this section that has very demand and is appreciated by clients as well if you provide the work with little efforts is "Whiteboard Animation". These are actually the videos where a hand is used to write a sequence of words or to draw an image just like an animation. What you need to do is just to install software "Video Scribe" and keep on playing with its different tools. Moreover, you can watch its tutorial at the start. After sometime, you will observe that you will get a command about that software and it is very easy to use. This software does not require more time and you can even finish one gig service within an hour.

FIVERR101 JPIZZ

You will need to pay 25$ within a month in order to use this software but when you will observe that how much does it pay to you then you will not care about the price of this software. One thing about which you need to take great care is to learn about different tricks and tools of this softwares as much as you can because how much professional are you, will decide how much you can earn within a day. You can also hire someone else at low rates from other sites but you should be expert in dealing with this software by your own because it is very simple and it takes very less time to complete single gig service.

There are some other ways to earn through video editing section such as, you can edit a video and add different transitions and effects to make it more attractive. For this you can use a simple free software like "Video Pad" or if you want to be more professional then you can use "Camtasia Studio" which is a paid software but it will give you too much within a short time. It will not take greater proportion of your time but you can easily learn about it after giving some time to it. The user may ask to cut some portion of video, add different effects or to change the background music and you can easily do it through any of these softwares. In return, you will get a 5$ for each small amount of work with an extra five star rating and a good review. So, you have no need to hire any of the client from other sites in this area and you can easily be expert in this field after giving some time to these softwares.

Programming and Tech

This section is considered to be as the most complicated if you are not familiar with this field but some sub-categories of this section can give you a good earning. It is not only limited with the programming of a single subject but you can easily earn a lot of money if you are familiar with any one language of programming like C++, Java, PHP, MATLAB and arduino programming. The only reason due to which many top rated sellers chose this section is because you have no need to write too much about this gig. You will just have to think and create a new idea according to the demand of the buyer and if you are able to do so, then it means you can easily write even 5 to 6 programs within an hour. One thing to be noted is that you should choose this field for your services if you are really expert in it because it requires the exercise of mind and you cannot even take too much help from online resources.

Another simple but important gig of this section is to convert one type of file into another type. For this, you have no need to do anything extra and you can install some important softwares for conversion or even some online sites also provide you an opportunity to convert your file from one type to another type. It will not even take your much time and you can simply convert more than 10 to 20 files within an hour or two. For each single conversion you can charge 5$ or you can increase the number of conversion per gig to attract the buyers towards your services.

How to Get Success at Each Step

Whenever you join Fiverr then it means you are now entered into a professional place where you will have to take everything in a serious way and try to deliver your services after working hard and in an honest way. If you will adopt any wrong way then you can even lose your account temporarily or permanently. Some important ways of promoting yourself and getting success through Fiverr are as follows:

→ First of all, whenever you will get a message at Fiverr for the first time or even the time when you are at level 1 or level 2 then you should deal with them in a good way. You should listen to their demands completely and then respond in a polite way even if you are ready to do that service or not because there may be the possibility that they get your service in some other time. Never try to ignore any single person on the Fiverr because if you will ignore someone or will not reply to that person then it will increase your response time (the time which will show how fast you reply to your clients) and which will reduce the chances of getting orders. Moreover, when you are working with a user then you should deal with him in a good way even if he/she asks you to change some points in your services that you have already provided because every single negative review can effect your earning and performance in a bad way.

→ The second and the most important thing is the time when you get your first order because it plays an important role in leaving your first impression infront of other buyers. You may find a little delay in getting your first order at Fiverr because it is very rare to give a chance to a new comer at the Fiverr but whenever you get a chance then you can easily prove your excellence after working hard and giving full time to the services about which the buyer is asking from you. Your first review may leave a good impression for your profile and it can give you a chance to get more orders easily. So, you must take it serious whenever you get it and do not mind if the buyer ask you to modify your work again because he/she will give you a good review once he/she is satisfied from your services.

→ When you start getting a lot of orders within a day then you have no need to react with every order because it may be difficult for you to deal with every user at Fiverr in an effective way. So, you need to focus at quality instead of quantity and if you are unable to manage time for any service or order at that time then you should respond to the buyer in such a way that he/she never get a poor impression from you. In this way, he/she will also understand that you are busy in some other stuff and it will not even decrease your rating. Otherwise, if you will simply ignore the messages coming from buyers then it may leave a poor impression about you in their minds which may effect you while working with them in future.

→ Whenever you are able to get enough orders each day at Fiverr then you should focus on developing repeat customers for you because it will create just like a good relationship between both of you as a buyer and seller. For this reason, you need to follow each customer after delivering your order and getting a good review. Follow up is a good thing to increase repeat customers because they always keep your excellence in mind and may contact you again whenever they want to get benefits from your services. There are more chancing of getting gig extras after working with repeat customers as they also take good care of your efforts and may even give you a tip whenever they are happy or satisfied from your services.

→ One more important thing about which you need to take great care is to deliver your every order on time. Take good care of time because it will also represent how much serious and responsible are you with your services. For this reason, you need to deliver every order before time because if you will deliver any order after creating a delay then it will leave a poor impression about your work in the customer's mind and there are less chances of getting good reviews and to increase the extent of repeat customers.

Summary

Fiverr is the best place for earning. Especially for those who are beginners and know nothing about different online marketing strategies and do not know how to resolve with online networking issues. You can easily start selling your gig at Fiverr from 5$ and then can earn a big amount ranging into thousands dollars within a month. You can easily join it if you have any single skill about which you are sure that you can attract others with your services. This is an important place where your experience adds up in the form of good reviews and your rating shows how much you are sincere with your work and how much others can trust at you before ordering your services. Although, there is no shortcut method or any wrong way of earning through Fiverr but you can even maximize your earning within minimum time depending upon the extent how much serious are you with your work. You should deal with every customer in a good way because every positive review increases the chance of getting more orders and every negative review may spoil your whole efforts. You have no need to involve in the gigs about which you do not know too much but you should focus yourself only at the services about which you know how to deliver them in an efficient way. This site can give you maximum earning within minimum time if you are serious with your work and deliver your every gig in a good way.

www.ingramcontent.com/pod-product-compliance
Lightning Source LLC
Chambersburg PA
CBHW040926180526
45159CB00002BA/632